THANK YOU

God, John Gray, Mothe
Humphrey, Happy, Cosmo and Willie.

Adolfo Monzon, Amanda Trevino, Amy Brown, Amy AL Gawlik, Anita Marley, Angela Hill, Anna Fugate-Downs, Ashley Thomas, Aubrey & Tami Rodgers, Azeneth Castillo, Baby Louis, Binky Morgan and Ron Anderson, Brandi Hartman, Brenda and Don Nugent, Brenda Klein, Brandon Castenada, Brooke Rogan, Bud and Karen Royer, Callisto Griffith, Candace Rothelle, Carlos Monzon, Celeste Campos, Chanda Hakanson, Charyl Coleman, Christopher Byman, Christina Blackledge, Coco Camacho, Cynthia Lively, Darwa Webb, David Cantu, Deborah Ragazzi, Deitra Ramos, Dixie Cohn, Donavon and Petra Frankenreiter, Edgar Camacho, Elizabeth Gilbert, Erica & Roger Facer, Eugenia Osbon, Eustolia Graham, Faith Scott, Fallon Orsdale, Flo Suttle, Gabby Monzon, Geet, Abhishek and Master Ji, Gina Galvan, Ginger Everett, Hilary Fornefeld, Hollie Fairchild, Ilce Maldonado, Inna Grudtcina, Jacinta Mack, Jamie and Casey Hislop, Jerriann McLauren, Jessie Trentacosta, Jill Elliott, Jim and Korky Fonder, Jo Packham, Joe Mays, Jorge Camacho, Julie Greenwood and John, Katie Olsen, Kelly Looney, Kevin Kibbie, Krista Morton, Linda Atkins, Linda Bow, Lindsey Dempsey, Lisa Granberg, Lisa Haradon, Loren Dempsey, Louis Castaneda, Lupita Aguilar, Macy Schulze, Madi Kimmel, Madisen Jacoby, Magdalena Alamaza, Marcine Garcia, Maria Contreas, Marisa and Eric Scott, Melissa Humphries, Mike Clark and Nancy Govro, Monica Rogan, Nana, Nichole Capsay, Nohemi Maldonado, Oksana Smetanuk, Palma Garnett, Pam Heinen, Pat Landes, Paul and Paul Jr. Hartcraft, Paula Monzon, Pedernales Veterinary Center, Preston Brown, Preston Brown Jr., Preston Gray, Ramona Lindscomb-Walker, Randy Siciliano, Rayna Halliburton, Rex & Kelly Foster, Rhonda Wilcox, Ricky Casteneda, Richard Casteneda, Robert, Kathleen, Clara and Chloe Keen, Rodney Bursiel, Ron Anderson, Sandy Whitehead, Sarah Kammlah, Saskia Thode, Shane Dyson, Sierra Jeffries, Stephanie Blummel, Steve Whyman & Emily Cowart, Tammy Browning-Smith, Tara and Nate Kelley, Thovas and Tina Brown, Tim, Carol, Mac & Augusta Bolton, Todd Hallmark, Tony and Yesica Castaneda, Tony Scott, Treva Collins, Valorie Mitchell, Verna Lee Cummings-Cuellar, Victoria Erickson, Whitney Hill, Whoopi Goldberg, Winter Edwards, Yolanda De La Cruz, Yvonne Haug, The entire Magnolia Pearl Family, Our Beautiful Town of Fredericksburg, Luckenbach, Bandera TX, Marburger Farm Antique Show, Marburger Family and Posse, Loyal Friends, Followers, and Lovers of MP.

A SPECIAL THANKS TO CANDACE ROTHELLE, CHRIS BYMAN, ERICA FACER, JOE MAYS, JOHN GRAY AND LINDSEY DEMPSEY FOR THEIR TIME AND DEDICATION TO MAKING THIS BOOK A REALITY.

FOREWORD

WHAT HAPPENS WHEN YOU HAVE AN OLD SOUL WITH NEW IDEAS

WHAT HAPPENS WHEN YOUR IDEAS NEVER SHUT OFF IN YOUR MIND

WHAT HAPPENS WHEN YOU BELIEVE THAT LOVE CAN CONQUER ALL

WHAT HAPPENS WHEN YOU BELIEVE IN THE PAST SO MUCH YOU MAKE IT A PART OF YOUR FUTURE

WHAT HAPPENS WHEN YOU BELIEVE FRIENDS ARE MORE VALUABLE THAN ALL THE MONEY IN THE WORLD

WHAT HAPPENS WHEN YOUR DREAMS BECOME REALITY

WHAT HAPPENS WHEN YOUR FAMILY BECOMES BIGGER THAN YOUR BLOODLINE

WHAT HAPPENS WHEN MUSIC IS YOUR RELIGION

WHAT HAPPENS WHEN YOU BELIEVE WE ARE ALL ONE

WHAT HAPPENS WHEN PEOPLE WEAR THE ART YOU CREATE

WHAT HAPPENS WHEN STARS COLLIDE

WHAT HAPPENS WHEN LAUGHTER BECOMES YOUR MEDICINE

WHAT HAPPENS WHEN YOU CLOSE YOUR EYES AT NIGHT BUT STILL SEE EVERYTHING

WHAT HAPPENS WHEN YOU GIVE MORE THAN YOU TAKE

WHAT HAPPENS WHEN YOU'RE TRAVELING WITHOUT MOVING

WHAT HAPPENS WHEN YOU BELIEVE IN MAGIC

YOU MAKE MAGNOLIA PEARL...

— DONAVON FRANKENREITER

...AND THE STARS GO WITH YOU

by Robin Brown

PHOTOGRAPHY BY JOANNA MACLENNAN,
RODNEY BURSIEL & CHRISTOPHER BYMAN
TEXT BY ROBIN BROWN & JESS BRASHER

"Allow beauty to shatter you regularly. The loveliest people are the ones who have been burnt, broken, and torn at the seams, yet still send their open hearts into the world to mend with love again, and again, and again, and again. You must allow yourself to feel your life while you're in it."
-Victoria Erickson

The root of the word "journey" shares its Latin origin with the word for one's daily portion: "diurnal". Though they may seem unrelated, their mutual source suggests a thread joining the small things we do each day to the overarching theme of these days sewn together. The smallest rituals become expansive—the tiniest details woven into a tapestry.

My journey started on September 28th, 1963. I entered this world two months early, high on Peyote and addicted to heroin. If a woman is a vessel and a child a blank slate, my mother's pain patina'd me from the get-go. There is no map for any of our lives, and my mother, Anna, was adrift. Amidst the substances she absorbed (that, in turn, absorbed her) and at sea with motherhood at 26, Anna treaded water the best she could. I, both her anchor and her lifeguard, bobbed alongside—grateful for the opportunity to swim at all. I loved her fiercely.

My father was my jetty in this sea. Imperfect and addicted, he nonetheless provided a place for me to lay my soul on the rocks and breathe—peek between the cracks and find little pools teeming with life. Our family moved to Hollywood, CA soon after my birth so my mother could further her career as a prostitute. The demands of her lifestyle meant I spent most of my early years with my father, who became my greatest teacher and my best friend—truly my soul human.

While I plan to write a book about this life of mine, of ours, for now I can say my journey has been filled with: tcreativity, adversity, pain, art, motion, loss, deep conversation, color, grief, resilience, generosity, service, awareness, tears, gratitude, deep sadness, laughter and forgiveness. I am a work in progress—we all are. I would like to believe my greatest gifts—compassion, generosity, forgiveness and love—are culled from hours, days, years and decades of pain transformed into wisdom and awareness.

Creativity saved my life.
The ability to love saves me every day.

"If you knew what I know about the power of giving, you would not let a single meal pass without sharing in some way"
-Buddha

God was so gracious to gift us this life and though it is sometimes unbearable, it is often quite beautiful. How can we ever repay such a gift? Are we supposed to? I come from the belief that we should always pay it forward.

My childhood was marked by a lack of material things—even food was scarce. My brother and I were frequently hungry. We foraged pecans from a tree in our backyard and water from the neighbors' garden hose as we waited for our mom to return from her all-too-frequent drinking binges. Sometimes it was three weeks before she reappeared to collect the food stamps, sell half of them to buy alcohol, and get us groceries with the rest.

We were rich, too, however—the wealth of wisdom and appreciation bestowed upon us by our father, Preston, taught us to find the lesson in all situations—to seek the good. He intoned that pain is often our greatest teacher and that the only way to keep going is through love and generosity. When he died years later, a quote in the sketchbook on his nightstand put it simply:

"A poor man shames us all...Do you like my song? I'll sing it for you"
-Unknown

PRESTON BROWN

STUDY OF MY LEFT HAND 1969

Preston believed that no matter how small, we all have something to give. Each day is the perfect day to share your light.

This spirit of simple generosity is the foundation of Magnolia Pearl. "No one has ever become poor by giving," wrote Anne Frank, and, indeed, any success our company has enjoyed flows from this well. As a well gives water it also draws water—such is the energetic exchange of a gift, any gift.

"The gift moves towards the empty place. As it turns in its circle it turns towards him who has been empty-handed the longest, and if someone appears elsewhere whose need is greater, it leaves its old channel and moves towards him."
-Lewis Hyde

If we become afraid to give—be it money or time, effort or love—we block the exchange, get lost from source. It is a bit like a kink in a hose: you expend more effort twisting yourself into a knot, holding back what is meant to flow, and for what? So that you may have more? So that you may not lack? Nothing else in nature behaves this way. A flower blooms, a bird chirps, the sun rises—all of this whether we are there to watch or not.

It is simple to say but often difficult to practice this in our society. We have been conditioned to fear lack, but those who have experienced scarcity know the real danger is poverty of spirit. And those suffering spiritual shortage most need those gifts that are free: a song, a shoulder, a smile. Don't be afraid to give or share. You never know the impact of the smallest gesture.

Where we come from is important, but it does not define us or keep us from our purpose. Some specifics of every journey are predetermined, but how the journey is perceived—how it is shared—is the art of becoming. The stamps on life's passport might read "abuse", "poverty", "addiction". But these are only words, not sentences.

I have always been grateful for our Magnolia Pearl family—we have been so blessed. It is from this place of deep tgratitude that I share this. Our entire operation started with one handmade purse, a simple thing stitched together from a place of poverty and exhaustion. But it was also a place of hope. This first piece was woven from the same thread I've sewn my heart back together with again, and again, and again—the hope of transformation, of sharing, of being of service.

"You begin the poem by placing your thumb on the burn.
Then you stay until you are the shape of the fire that traveled you."
-Victoria Erickson

The fire that traveled me, that travels many of us, is enough to burn down the world. Harnessed and tended to, it is the beginning of all creative acts. We each carry the flame of our ancestors; each of our vessels have drops of their essence. Be they angels or demons or something in between, we get to be the alchemists.

Magnolia Pearl is the dream of my grandparents, my parents and then me. It is a dream built on overcoming, becoming, forgiveness and love. But most of all, God.

God means something different for everyone. Success means something different for everyone. I am here today to tell you that when you align your heart with gratitude and humility, almost anything is possible. Everything you need to succeed in this life is already here. By accepting this truth my life has transformed in more ways than I can count. Dedication and hard work are just part of the story. So many of us are dedicated and work hard, and it doesn't seem to be enough. That was me. It wasn't until the death of both of my parents that I started to see how practicing forgiveness and grace, letting go, trusting, was starting to change my life for the better.

We only have one job—to love. Actually, we have two jobs—to love and to shine. Don't let the pain of this world steal your sparkle. We come from light, we come here to shine and then we return to eternal light. Shine fearlessly and glow from your soul.

LOVE, ROBIN

"THIS IS EMPATHY: LET ME HOLD THE DOOR FOR YOU. I MAY HAVE NEVER WALKED A MILE IN YOUR SHOES, BUT I CAN SEE YOUR SOLES ARE WORN, YOUR STRENGTH IS TORN UNDER THE WEIGHT OF A STORY I HAVE NEVER LIVED BEFORE. BUT LET ME HOLD THE DOOR FOR YOU. AFTER ALL YOU'VE WALKED THROUGH, IT'S THE LEAST I CAN DO."

-MORGAN HARPER NICHOLS

4

"What is Done in Love is done Well."

-Vincent Van Gogh

"GENIUS MIGHT BE THE ABILITY TO SAY A PROFOUND THING IN A SIMPLE WAY."
— CHARLES BUKOWSKI

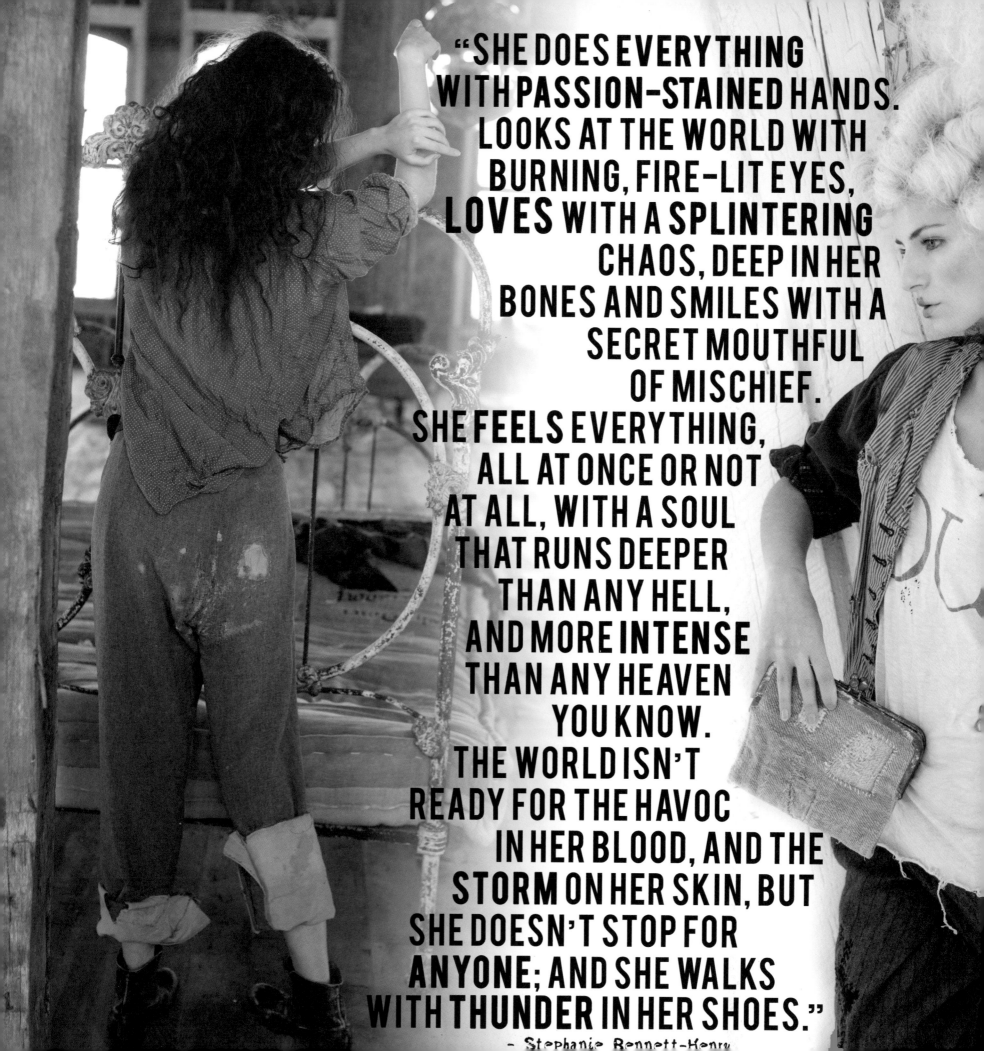

"SHE DOES EVERYTHING WITH PASSION-STAINED HANDS. LOOKS AT THE WORLD WITH BURNING, FIRE-LIT EYES, LOVES WITH A SPLINTERING CHAOS, DEEP IN HER BONES AND SMILES WITH A SECRET MOUTHFUL OF MISCHIEF. SHE FEELS EVERYTHING, ALL AT ONCE OR NOT AT ALL, WITH A SOUL THAT RUNS DEEPER THAN ANY HELL, AND MORE INTENSE THAN ANY HEAVEN YOU KNOW. THE WORLD ISN'T READY FOR THE HAVOC IN HER BLOOD, AND THE STORM ON HER SKIN, BUT SHE DOESN'T STOP FOR ANYONE; AND SHE WALKS WITH THUNDER IN HER SHOES."

- Stephanie Bennett-Henry

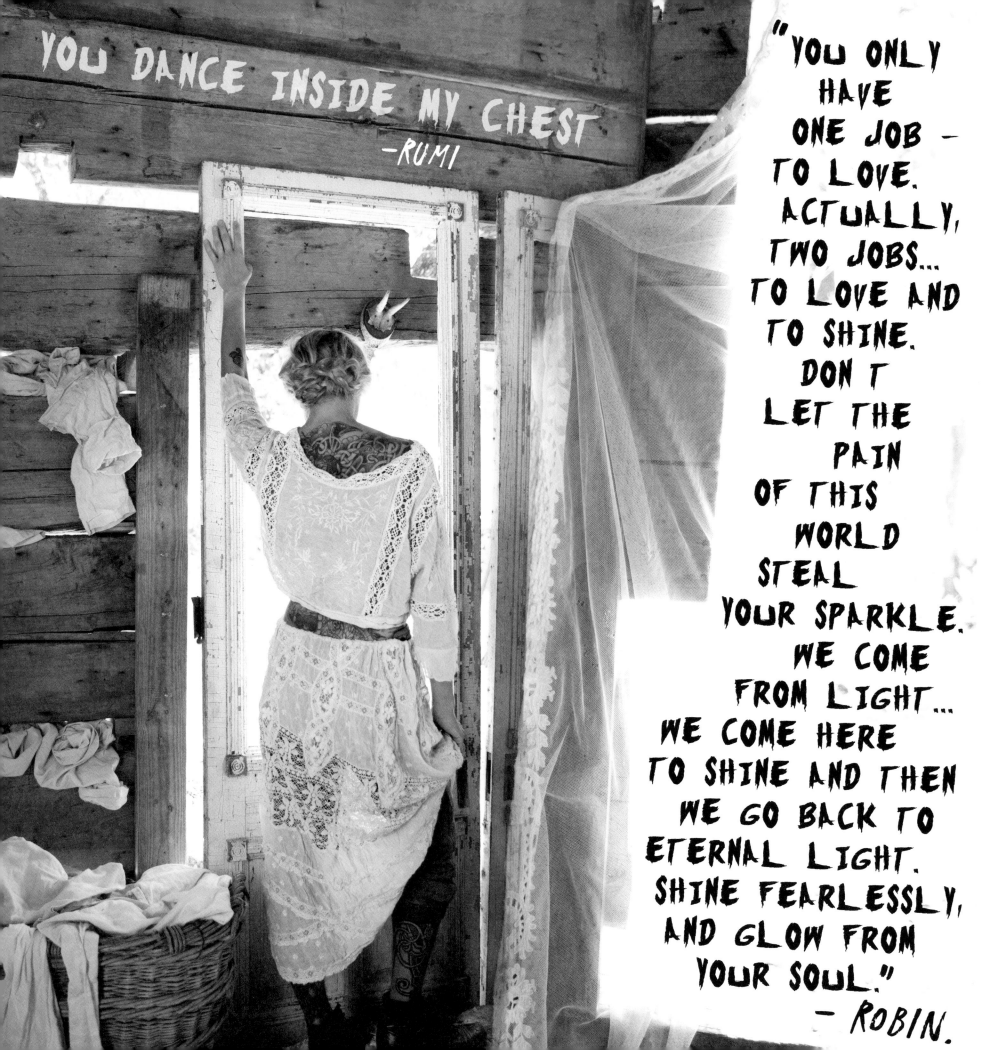

YOU DANCE INSIDE MY CHEST
—RUMI

"YOU ONLY HAVE ONE JOB — TO LOVE. ACTUALLY, TWO JOBS... TO LOVE AND TO SHINE. DON'T LET THE PAIN OF THIS WORLD STEAL YOUR SPARKLE. WE COME FROM LIGHT... WE COME HERE TO SHINE AND THEN WE GO BACK TO ETERNAL LIGHT. SHINE FEARLESSLY, AND GLOW FROM YOUR SOUL."
— ROBIN.

"TOO MANY WOMEN
WANTING TO
BE THE MUSE.
(YOU ARE THE POET)"

- LAUREN EDEN

"DON'T YOU KNOW YET?
IT IS YOUR LIGHT THAT
LIGHTS THE WORLD."
— RUMI

26

"SHE ISN'T HUMAN;
SHE IS ART,
WITH A HEART."

- j. iron word

"I DID NOT COME TO TEACH YOU.
I CAME TO LOVE YOU.
LOVE WILL TEACH YOU."

"The essence of all beautiful ART, all great ART is GRATITUDE."

—friedrich nietzsche

"Simplicity is the
final achievement
after one has
played a VAST
quantity of notes
and more notes,
it is SIMPLICITY
that emerges
as the crowning
reward of ART."

-Frederic
Chopin

38

"IF IT IS ART,
IT IS NOT FOR ALL,
AND IF IT IS FOR ALL,
IT IS NOT ART."
- Arnold Schoenberg

"There is only one real happiness in life, and that is the happiness of creating."

-frederick delius

"i should be sorry if i only entertained them. i wish to make them better."
-george frederic handel

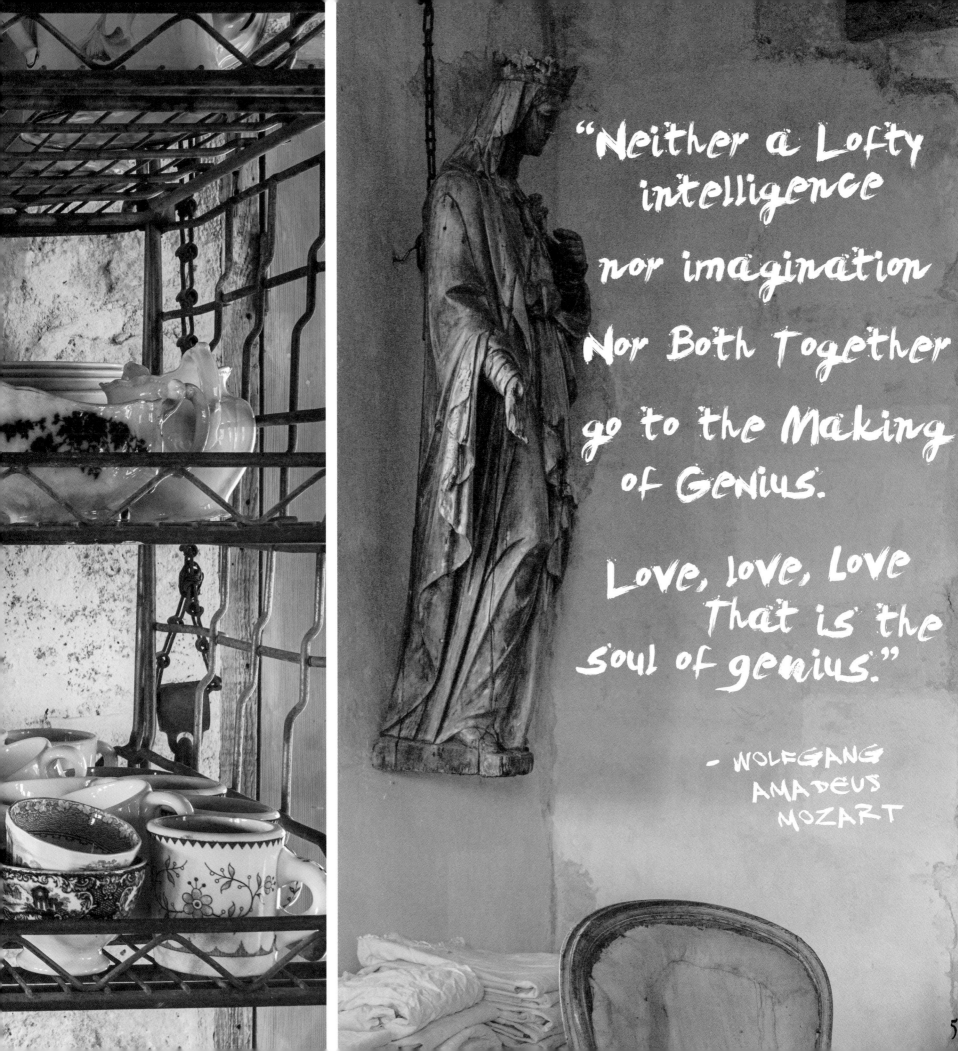

"Neither a lofty intelligence nor imagination Nor both together go to the making of Genius.

Love, love, Love That is the soul of genius."

— WOLFGANG AMADEUS MOZART

52

"I will not be another flower, picked for my BEAUTY and left to die. I will be WILD, difficult to find, and impossible to forget."
— Erin Van Vuren

"I KNOW NOTHING WITH ANY CERTAINTY, BUT THE SIGHT OF THE STARS MAKES ME DREAM."
—Vincent Van Gogh

WE MUST...

"WE MUST BRING OUR OWN
LIGHT TO THE DARKNESS."
- CHARLES BUKOWSKI

"FROM THE MOMENT I HELD THE BOX OF COLORS IN MY HAND, I KNEW THIS WAS MY LIFE.

- Henri Matisse

"IT'S NOT HOW MUCH WE GIVE BUT HOW MUCH LOVE WE PUT INTO GIVING."

- MOTHER TERESA

"WHEN WE LISTEN TO CERTAIN
TYPES OF MUSIC OR SOAK
OUR EYES WITH PAINTINGS
IT ALL BEGINS TO BLEND AND RUN
THROUGH US, QUIETLY BECOMING
PART OF OUR BLOOD, FLESH AND BONES.
WE ALWAYS CARRY THE ART WE'VE LOVED"

-victoria erickson

"MINDFULNESS GIVES US THE POWER TO UNDERSTAND OUR DEEP CONNECTION WITH THE TREES, FLOWERS, STARS, SUN, AND THE MOON."

- AMIT RAY

"THE SINGING SUN,
THE SINGING MOON,
THE SINGING STARS
AND THE SINGING
GALAXIES ARE THE
DIRECT EXPRESSION
OF THE DIVINE WORD
AUM."

— AMIT RAY

"ONE MUST ASK CHILDREN AND BIRDS HOW

CHERRIES AND STRAWBERRIES TASTE."

— JOHANN
WOLFGANG VON
GOETHE

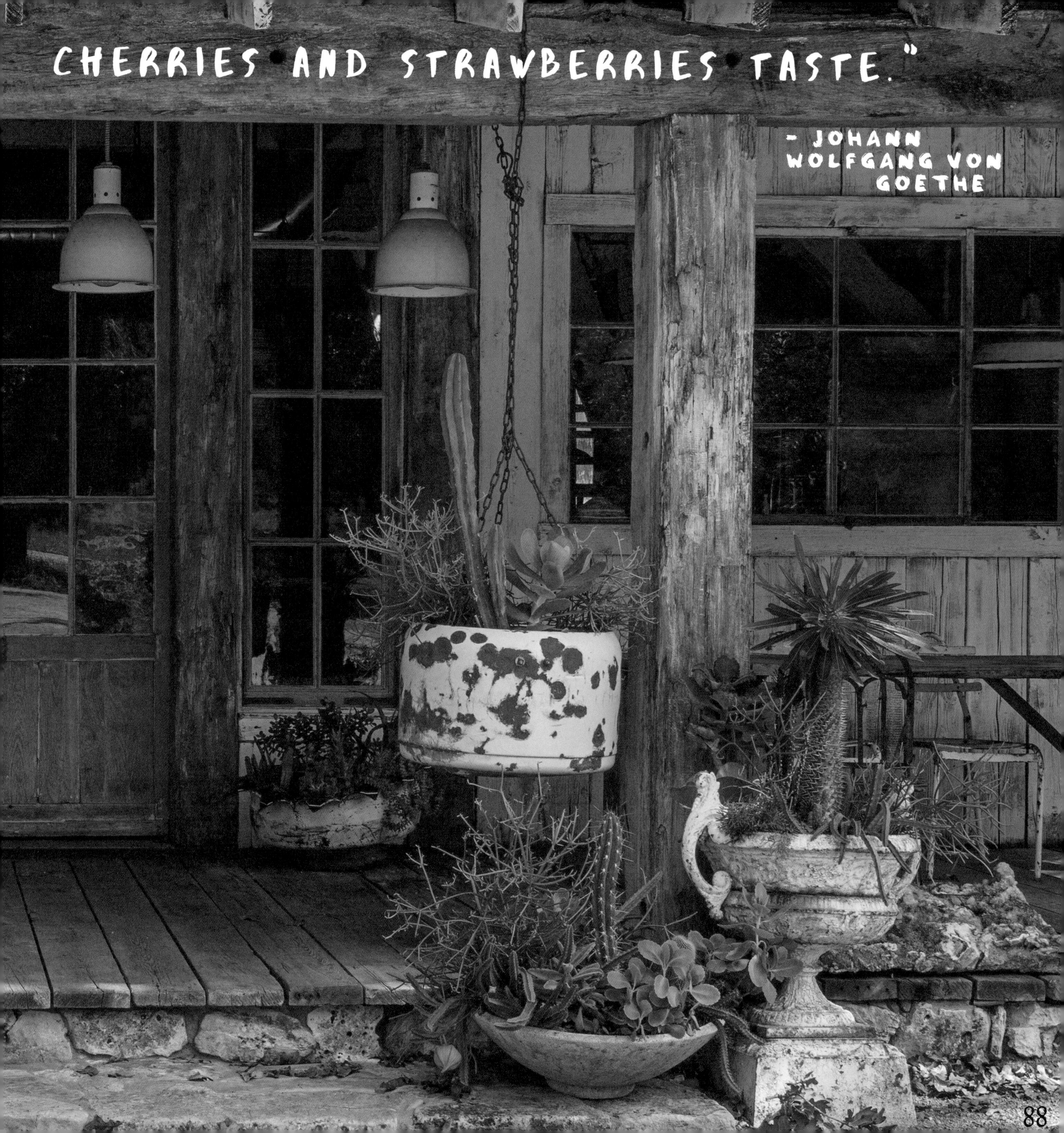

"YOU'RE ONLY GIVEN A
LITTLE SPARK OF MADNESS.
YOU MUSTN'T LOSE IT."
— ROBIN WILLIAMS

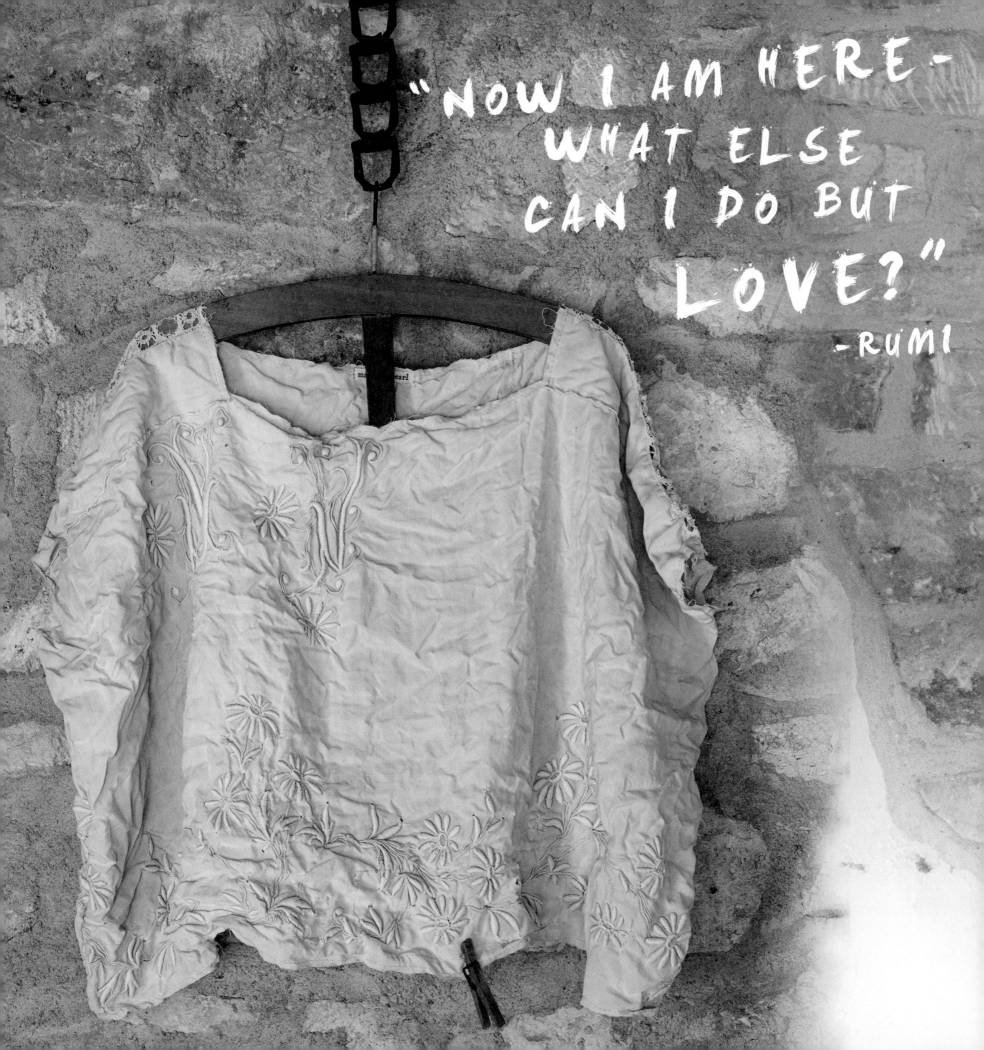

"NOW I AM HERE -
WHAT ELSE
CAN I DO BUT
LOVE?"
-RUMI

"I CAN ONLY CONNECT DEEPLY OR NOT AT ALL."

- Anaïs Nin

"ART (LIKE LOVE) WAS NEVER ABOUT SAFETY. TO LOVE AN ARTIST IS TO FALL INTO A SEA OF DEEP, SOULFUL, COURAGEOUS, WILD LIVING."

— VICTORIA ERICKSON

"PROMISE TO STAY WILD WITH ME. WE'LL SEEK AND RETURN AND STAY AND FIND BEAUTY AND THE EXTRAORDINARY IN ALL THE SPACES WE CAN CLAIM. WE'LL KNOW HOW TO LIVE. HOW TO BREATHE MAGIC INTO THE MUNDANE."

-VICTORIA ERICKSON

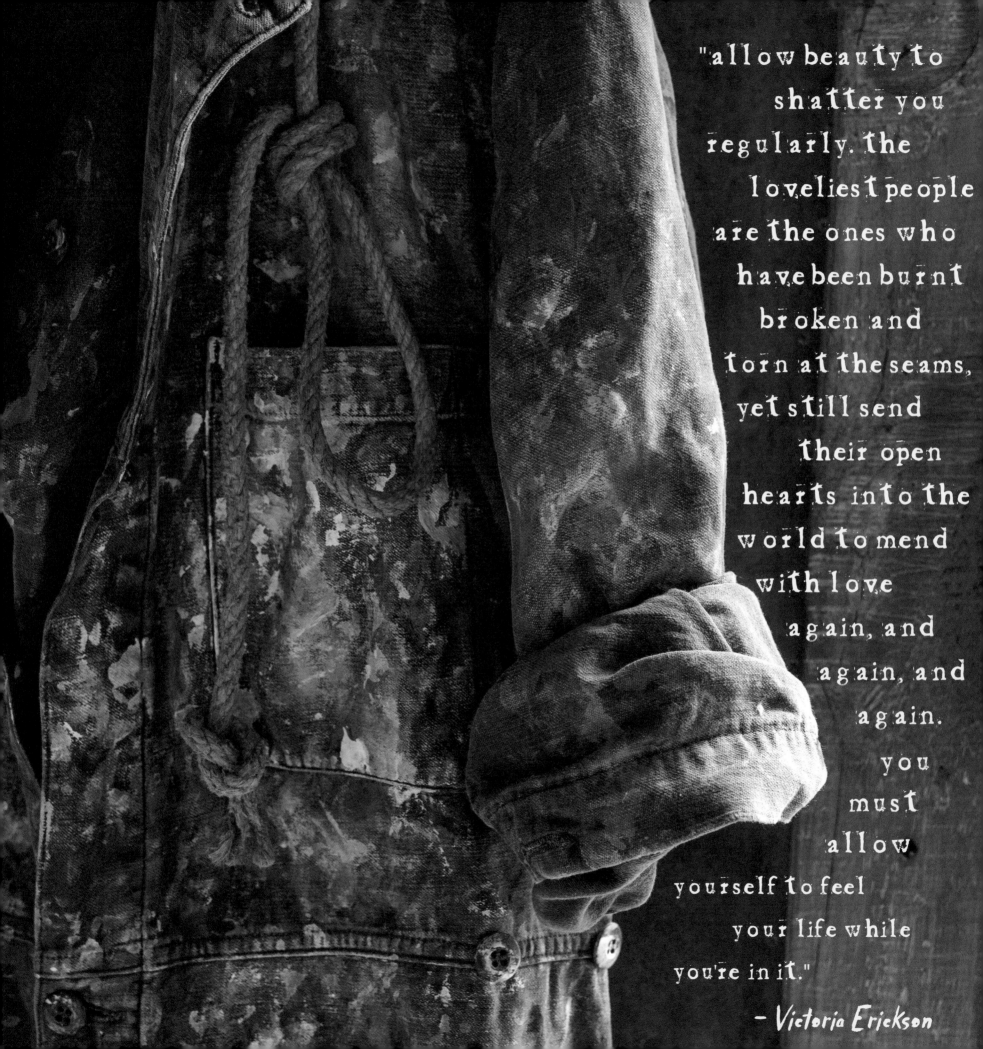

"allow beauty to shatter you regularly. the loveliest people are the ones who have been burnt broken and torn at the seams, yet still send their open hearts into the world to mend with love again, and again, and again. you must allow yourself to feel your life while you're in it."

— Victoria Erickson

"If there is light it will find you"
—Charles Bukowski

"NO ONE EVER BECAME POOR FROM GIVING."

– ANNE FRANK

108

"THE WORLD IS
FULL OF MAGIC THINGS,
PATIENTLY WAITING
FOR OUR SENSES
TO GROW SHARPER."

— W.B. YEATS

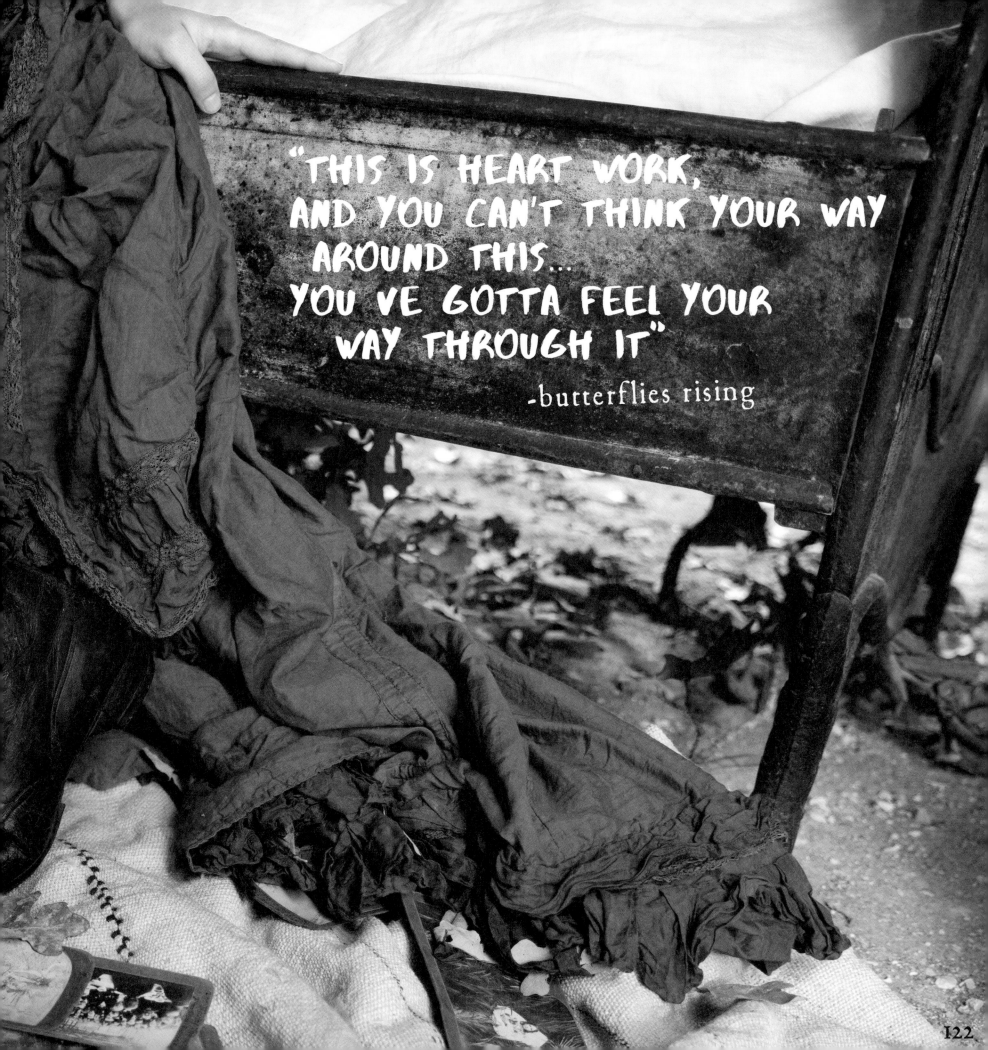

"THIS IS HEART WORK,
AND YOU CAN'T THINK YOUR WAY
AROUND THIS...
YOU'VE GOTTA FEEL YOUR
WAY THROUGH IT"

-butterflies rising

"FASHION IS MORE ART THAN ART IS."
- ANDY WARHOL

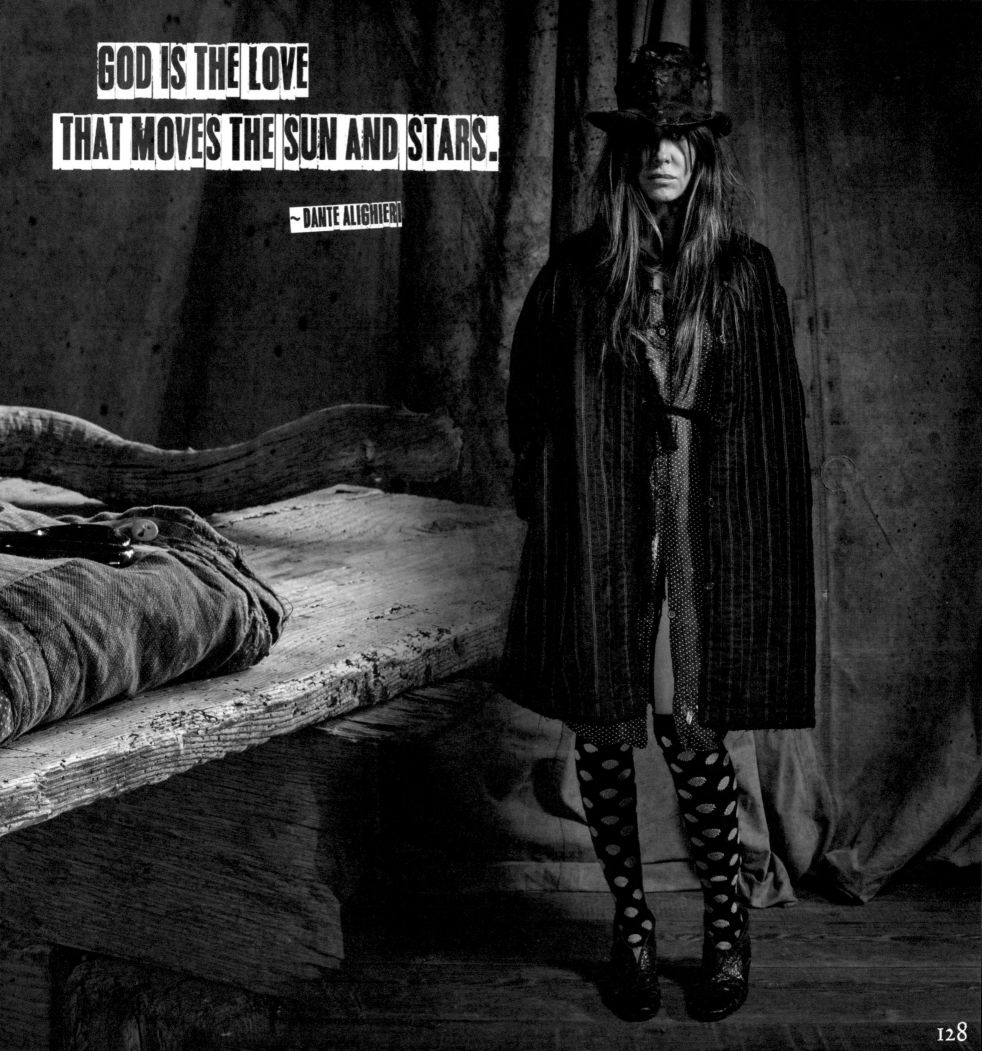

GOD IS THE LOVE
THAT MOVES THE SUN AND STARS.

~ DANTE ALIGHIERI

128

"WHEN THE POWER OF LOVE
OVERCOMES THE LOVE OF POWER,
THE WORLD WILL KNOW PEACE."
-JIMI HENDRIX

"IT IS NOT AN ARTIST'S JOB TO PLEASE ANYONE, BUT TO BRAVELY DO THE WORK THAT THEY ARE MOST COMPELLED TO DO. IT'S THE PUBLIC'S JOB TO BRAVELY SEEK OUT AND APPRECIATE THE WORK THAT RESONATES WITH THEM."

-STEVE PETERS

"SIMPLICITY IS THE DIRECT RESULT OF PROFOUND THOUGHT."

— ANONYMOUS

"THE ROLE OF THE ARTIST IS EXACTLY
THE SAME AS THE ROLE OF THE LOVER.
IF I LOVE YOU, I HAVE TO MAKE YOU
CONSCIOUS OF THE THINGS YOU DON'T SEE."
-JAMES BALDWIN

Sell your books at
sellbackyourbooks at
Go to sellbackyourBook.com!
and get an sellbackyourBook.com
quote. We even instant price
shipping - see pay the
books are the
see what your old
books are worth your old
books are worth what your old
today!

Inspected By: ilda_hernandez

0 0 0 7 6 2 6 2 5 0 3

"WE ARE LIKE LICORICE. NOT EVERYBODY LIKES LICORICE, BUT THE PEOPLE WHO LIKE LICORICE REALLY LIKE LICORICE."

- Jerry Garcia

"We
Have Art
So
That We
Shall

Not Die
Of

Reality."

-Nietzsche

"DON'T ONLY PRACTICE YOUR ART, BUT FORCE YOUR WAY INTO ITS SECRETS, FOR IT AND KNOWLEDGE CAN RAISE MEN TO THE DIVINE." - *Ludwig Van Beethoven*

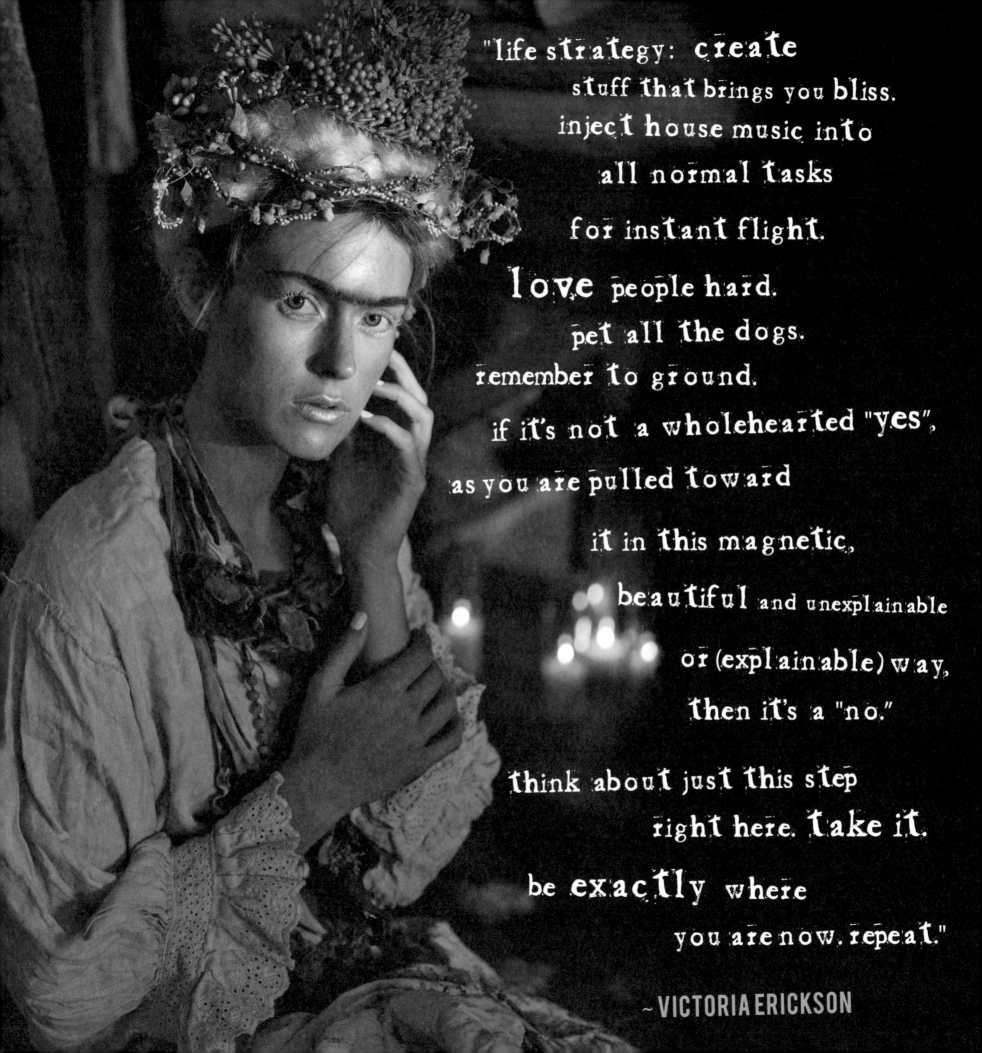

"life strategy: create
stuff that brings you bliss.
inject house music into
all normal tasks
for instant flight.
love people hard.
pet all the dogs.
remember to ground.
if it's not a wholehearted "yes",
as you are pulled toward

it in this magnetic,
beautiful and unexplainable
or (explainable) way,
then it's a "no."

think about just this step
right here. take it.
be exactly where
you are now. repeat."

~ VICTORIA ERICKSON

'I don't believe in magic.'
the young boy said. the old man smiled.
'you will when you see her.'

~atticus

"AND PERHAPS
WHAT MADE HER BEAUTIFUL
WAS NOT HER APPEARANCE
OR WHAT SHE ACHIEVED,
BUT IN HER LOVE
AND IN HER COURAGE,
AND HER AUDACITY
TO BELIEVE:
NO MATTER
THE DARKNESS
AROUND HER,
LIGHT RAN WILD
WITHIN HER, AND THAT
WAS THE WAY
SHE CAME ALIVE,
AND IT SHOWED UP
IN EVERYTHING."

- MORGAN
HARPER
NICHOLS

"YOU WILL NEVER BE ABLE TO ESCAPE FROM YOUR HEART. SO IT IS BETTER TO LISTEN TO WHAT IT HAS TO SAY."

— PAUL COELHO (THE ALCHEMIST)

"YOU HAVE TO PARTICIPATE RELENTLESSLY IN THE MANIFESTATION OF YOUR OWN BLESSINGS."

-Elizabeth Gilbert

"WHO BEING LOVED IS POOR?"
-OSCAR WILDE

"Just like a sunbeam can't separate itself from the sun, and a wave can't separate itself from the ocean, we can't separate ourselves from one another. We are all part of a vast sea of love, one indivisble divine mind."

-MARIANNE WILLIAMSON

"IF YOU KNEW WHAT I KNOW ABOUT THE **POWER** OF **GIVING**, YOU WOULD **NOT** LET A SINGLE MEAL PASS WITHOUT **SHARING** IT IN SOME WAY."

- BUDDHA

"BEAUTY IS NOT CAUSED. IT IS."

-EMILY DICKINSON

"THERE'S A BLUEBIRD IN MY HEART"
-CHARLES BUKOWSKI

"THE GREAT MIND KNOWS THE POWER OF GENTLENESS."
—ROBERT BROWNING

"THE TWO MOST IMPORTANT DAYS IN YOUR LIFE ARE THE DAY YOU WERE BORN AND THE DAY YOU FIGURE OUT WHY."

– MARK TWAIN

190

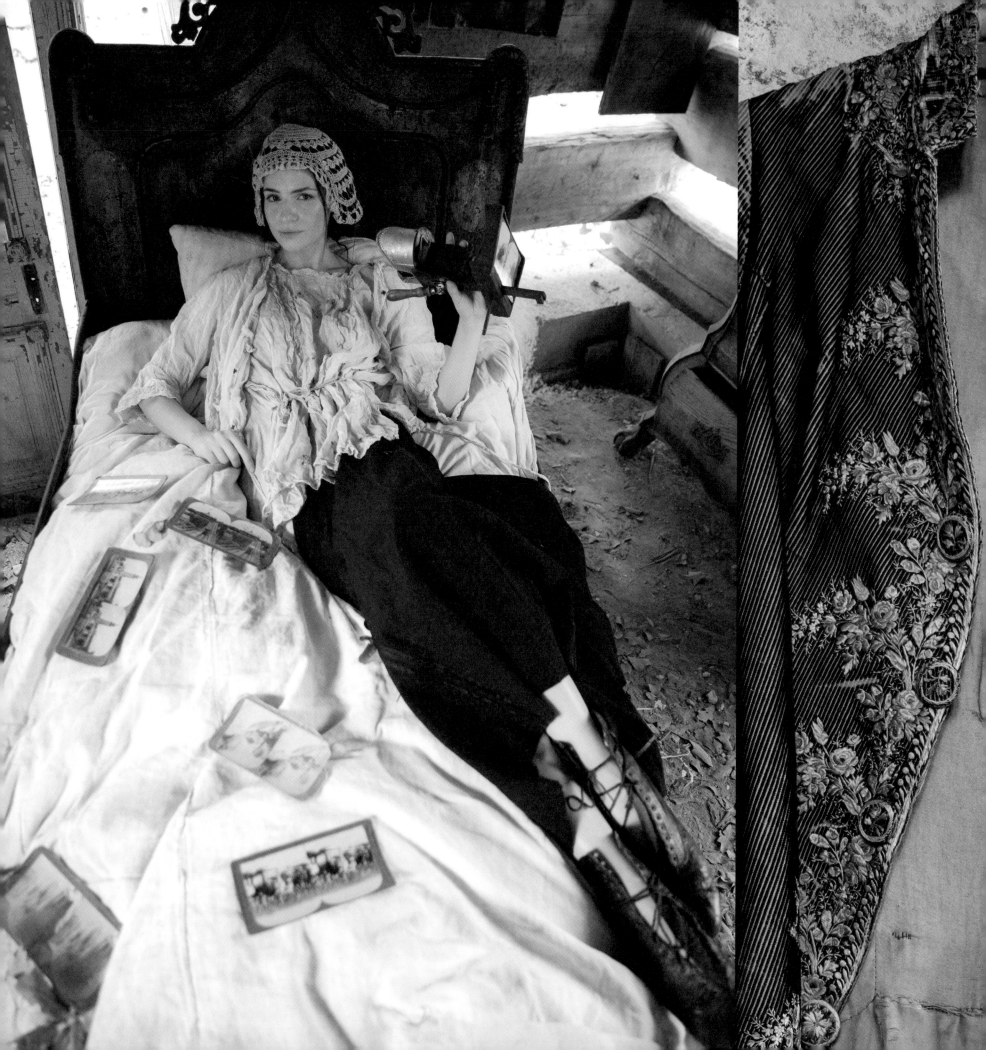

"ART IS AS NATURAL
AS SUNSHINE
AND AS VITAL
AS NOURISHMENT."
        —MARYANN F. KOHL

"I DON'T
WANT LIFE
TO IMITATE ART,
I WANT LIFE
TO BE ART."
— ERNEST
FISCHER

"HE WASN'T DOING A THING THAT I COULD SEE, EXCEPT STANDING THERE, LEANING ON THE BALCONY RAILING, HOLDING THE UNIVERSE TOGETHER."
—j.d. Salinger

AT NIGHT,
I OPEN THE
WINDOW AND
ASK THE MOON TO
COME AND PRESS
ITS FACE
AGAINST MINE.
BREATHE INTO ME.

-RUMI

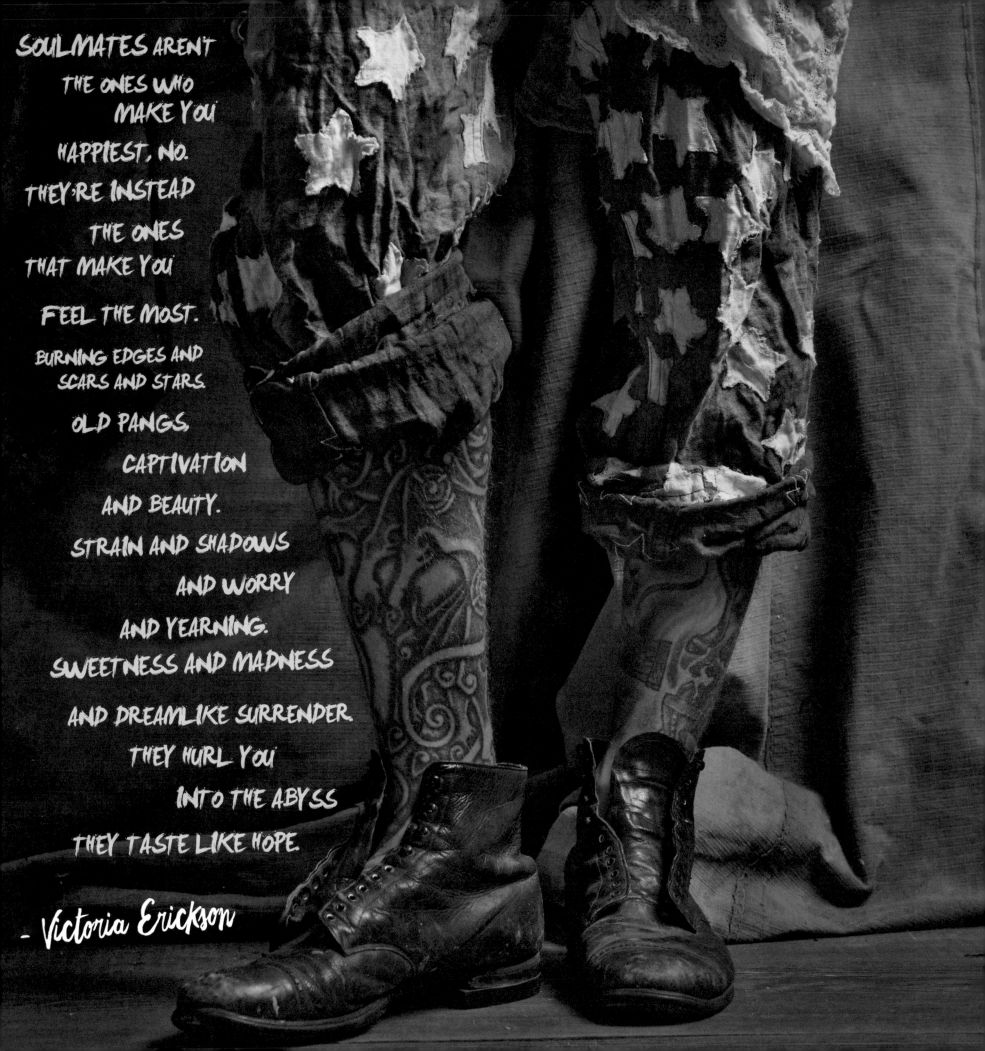

SOULMATES AREN'T
THE ONES WHO
MAKE YOU
HAPPIEST, NO.
THEY'RE INSTEAD
THE ONES
THAT MAKE YOU
FEEL THE MOST.
BURNING EDGES AND
SCARS AND STARS.
OLD PANGS,
CAPTIVATION
AND BEAUTY.
STRAIN AND SHADOWS
AND WORRY
AND YEARNING.
SWEETNESS AND MADNESS
AND DREAMLIKE SURRENDER
THEY HURL YOU
INTO THE ABYSS
THEY TASTE LIKE HOPE.

- Victoria Erickson

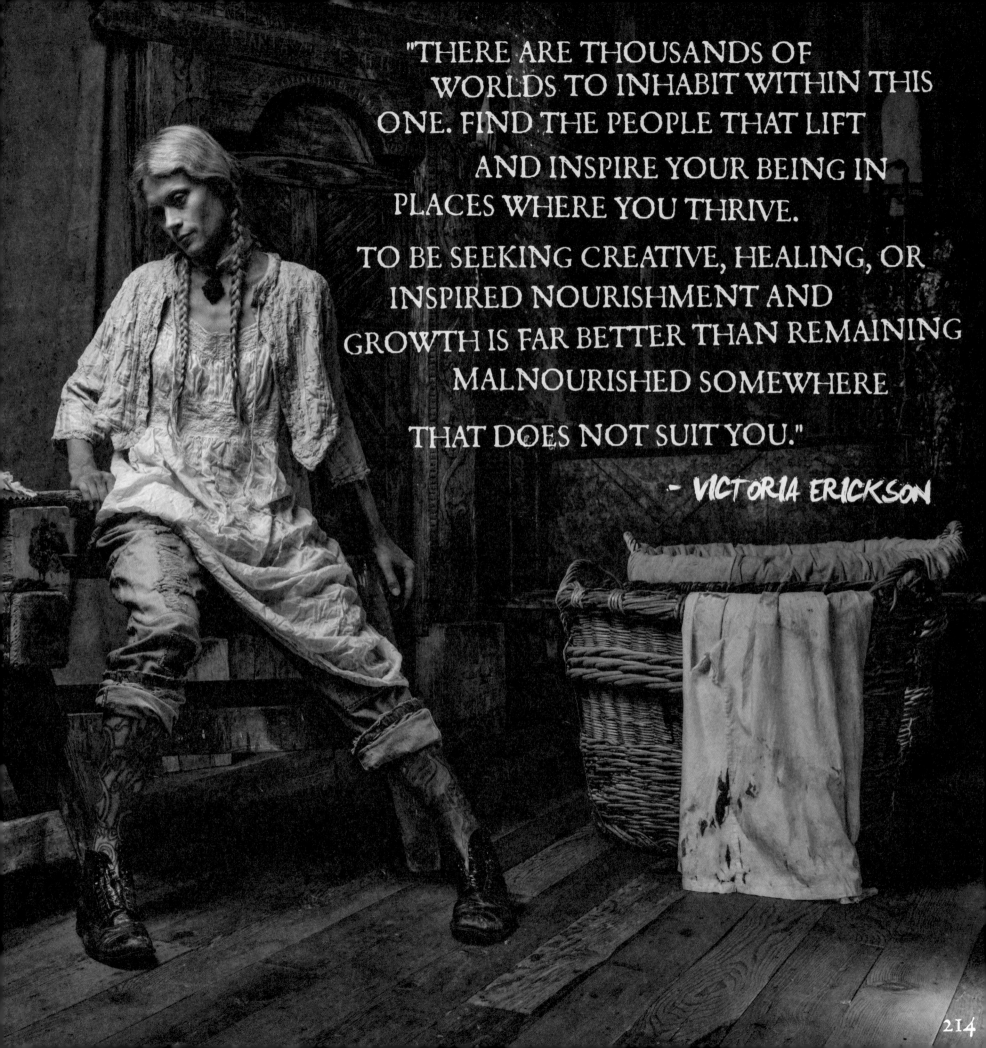

"THERE ARE THOUSANDS OF WORLDS TO INHABIT WITHIN THIS ONE. FIND THE PEOPLE THAT LIFT AND INSPIRE YOUR BEING IN PLACES WHERE YOU THRIVE.

TO BE SEEKING CREATIVE, HEALING, OR INSPIRED NOURISHMENT AND GROWTH IS FAR BETTER THAN REMAINING MALNOURISHED SOMEWHERE THAT DOES NOT SUIT YOU."

- VICTORIA ERICKSON

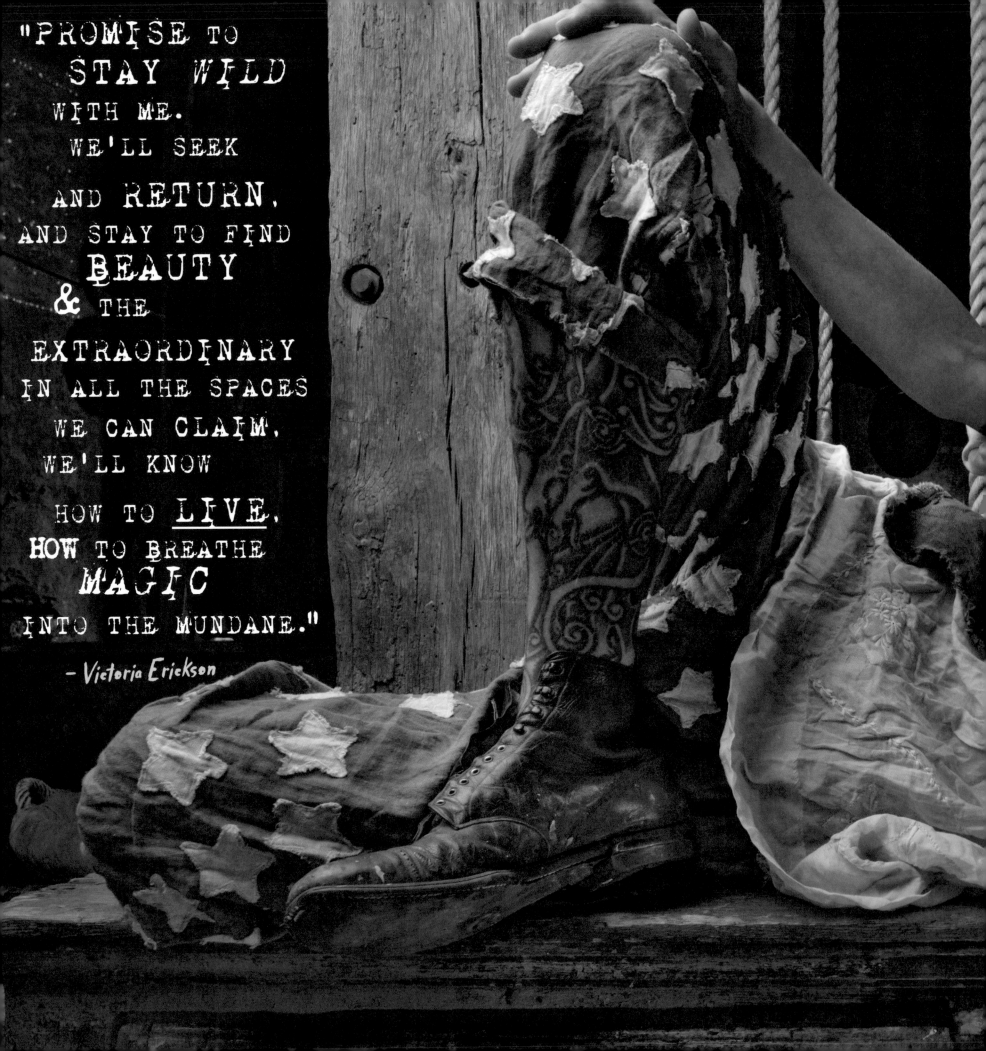

"PROMISE to STAY *WILD* WITH ME. WE'LL SEEK

AND RETURN, AND STAY TO FIND BEAUTY & THE EXTRAORDINARY IN ALL THE SPACES WE CAN CLAIM. WE'LL KNOW

HOW TO <u>LIVE</u>, HOW TO BREATHE MAGIC INTO THE MUNDANE."

— Victoria Erickson

"WHEN NIGHT FALLS, PEEL OFF YOUR SADNESS.

GIVE IT TO THE GALAXIES.
YOUR ORGANS WILL SHINE AGAIN BY SUNRISE.

THIS IS THE LANGUAGE OF FIRE."

— VICTORIA ERICKSON

"paradise has never been about places. it exists in moments. in connection. in flashes across time."

-Victoria Erickson